Weight Los

and Carb

MW00907196

Learn How to Overcome Sugar Addiction - A
Sugar Buster Super Detox Diet

Amazon Best Seller! ASIN: B00GUXOCNM

FREE Bonus Offer: free recipes

and other health and wellness

related books

Please Click Here for Instant Access to Free Recipe Book
http://www.healthylifenaturally.com/quitsugar/

ISBN-13:978-1494449285

ISBN-10:1494449285

Dedication

Dedicated to you, my dear reader and to your healthy habits. It is our sincere intention in writing this book to help you achieve your optimal health.

Copyright Notice

Publisher: Health Life Naturally
Author: Shawn Chhabra
Author: Milo E Newton
From an idea by: Shawn Chhabra
Editor: Jacqueline Harrington

Legal Disclaimer

Summary:

Most people know that sugar is not a very healthy food, but few understand that it is similar to some of the most potent drugs. Sugar can affect brain function, disrupt healthy metabolic processes, and cause substantial weight gain over only a short period of time.

Not only is it unhealthy, but it is almost unavoidable. Food growers and makers have been adding sugar to almost every imaginable food and beverage since the 1970s (including baby formula), and today it is a leading contributor to the obesity epidemic as well as many chronic diseases.

In "Weight Loss by Quitting Sugar and Carb - A Sugar Buster Super Detox Diet" you will learn all about sugar in the modern diet. Not only will you discover why sugar appears as widely as it does in the food supply, but you will learn the many reasons that you should cut it from your diet.

Readers will learn about:

- Sugar addiction and how it is a real problem;
- Added sugar and how it is not needed in food or the human metabolism;
- How sugar behaves in the body;
- How the body can work better without any added sugars;
- The best foods to choose in order to lose weight and avoid disease;
- Simple carbohydrates, hidden sugars, and artificial sweeteners are all unhealthy and should also be cut from the diet;
- Doing a true 21 Day Detox Diet;
- What to expect when cutting sugar from your lifestyle;

- Conquering the biggest challengers to sugar detox and elimination; and
- The various conspiracy theories and widespread efforts to keep sugar on our plates, in our drinks, and flooding our bodies.

When you have finished reading this book you will not only be happy to eliminate sugar from your daily diet, but will also know exactly what steps to take to ensure success. If you are ready to end your addiction to sugar, improve your health, and optimize your body's fat burning capabilities, this is the perfect guide.

"Healthy citizens are the greatest asset any country can have."
— Winston Churchill

Table of Contents

Introduction

According to many studies, the average American will eat around 19 teaspoons of sugar per day. That is just a bit less than 1/2 cup measure of sugar every single day! That also translates to 285 calories per day as well.

Obviously, this means that by cutting sugar calories out of your diet you can start to shed a few extra pounds in only a short amount of time. However, and this is a pretty substantial "however", there are a lot of ways that sugar sneaks into the diet and causes a lot of trouble besides weight gain.

For instance, there are foods that have the same effects of plain, old fashioned sugar. These foods also increase "blood sugar", trigger the production of certain hormones, and cause a reaction in the brain that is the same as consuming sugar. These foods are known as "simple carbohydrates" and eating them can cause you to crave more sugar, gain weight, and even experience some of the emotional impacts of a high sugar diet.

Examples of them include processed sugars such as corn syrup and pastas, or whole foods such as potatoes or rice. The interesting thing to know is that sugar and foods that create similar effects in the body can cause you to enter into a very fixed pattern or cycle. This is a cycle that is defined by craving and consuming sugar, feeling highs and lows caused by the body's reaction to sugar, and by weight gain due to the storage of empty sugar calories. Some call it a sugar cycle, but many health and food experts call it part of SAD or the Standard American Diet.

It is a pattern you may have unwittingly entered into early in life, and yet it is one that can be broken. In fact, it *should* be broken simply because sugar is a remarkably unhealthy material to consume. It is not natural - even when packaged as organic or "all natural" because it has to be heavily processed to reach the "sugar" state. That means it is void of most nutrients.

The biggest problem with eating sugar, however, and this applies to an enormous number of people, is that it becomes an addiction. You really can develop an eating disorder or really challenging eating habits associated with sugar. This might mean:

- You lose control of yourself as soon as you eat sugary foods;

- You go from not hungry to starving in only short periods of time;

- You feel badly or "low" if you don't eat some sort of sugar every day - this can include "brain fog" or fatigue, to sadness and anxiety;

- You reach automatically for a sugary or starchy food when tired or feeling an energy low; or

- You feel really shaky when you don't consume sugary foods during the day.

Additionally, a major sign that you are addicted to sugar is the fact that you just cannot seem to lose weight. This is often due to the fact that you are a sugar cycle eater who is relying on carbohydrates from sugar for energy rather than your body's preferred fuel - healthy fat.

Often, all of these issues are due to one thing - you are struggling to shake sugar or carbohydrate addiction.

A New Beginning

This book is going to introduce you to the basics of sugar addiction, and then walk you through a simple "detox diet" that will cut your sugar cravings for good. The diet will work in the simplest way possible - you will cut out all forms of simple sugar and carbohydrates for a very fixed period of time. After that time has come and gone, without you slipping up and eating sugar, you will find that your old sugar habit has been slain or at least dramatically reduced.

Naturally, you are going to experience a lot of different things during a detox period, including some rapid weight loss, some serious challenges in terms of energy and emotions, and some radical dietary changes. For example, if you are used to a bagel and OJ for breakfast, you might have difficulty adjusting to an egg white omelet and bacon instead. You might wonder where you'll get energy without the "zip" that comes from a straight shot of sugary sweet OJ.

Here's the thing: the fat and protein in the bacon give you pure energy in the form of dietary fat while that juice gives your body a fairly harmful blast of sucrose and glucose that it won't manage that well. This is why you'd be pretty tired mid-morning after that OJ and bagel, but why you'll feel clear headed and pretty energetic after that egg and bacon. However, once you break the sugar cycle, you will really start to crave this new diet because of the way it makes you feel - and look.

During the true sugar detox, you will be able to cleanse the body of a lot of stored carbs, improve the rate of your metabolism, and establish a set of new and healthier habits. So, let's start with a look at the "how and why" of sugar addiction and the reasons that this cycle is tougher to break than one might think.

"If we are creating ourselves all the time, then it is never too late to begin creating the bodies we want instead of the ones we mistakenly assume we are stuck with."
— Deepak Chopra

Chapter One

Sugar Addiction Explained

We know that most people consume that 1/2 cup or so of sugar every day. This is an amount that has increased substantially over time. Consider that a human being in the year 1800 would eat around 18 pounds of sugar every year (sounds like a lot doesn't it?), but that same person in the year 2010 was eating around 180 pounds in that same space of time!

And the sugars of 2010 are radically different from those of 1910, and not in good ways.

Why on earth are we eating so much of this stuff?

- *Because we want it.*

- *We want it because we have developed addictions to it (and for some of us this addiction began with our first bottle of baby formula).*

- *We want sugar because it is marketed to us by "big business".*

- *And because it is the massive commercial food industry that adds sugar to foods that we don't even know contain sugar.*

We are going to look at all of these issues, but for now, let's just consider how sugar gets into our bodies and our diets.

Sugar in the Modern Diet

As an example, over the past forty years added sugars have started to appear in:

- Baby foods and formulas;

- Salad dressings and marinades;

- Crackers;

- Processed cheeses;

- Canned sauces and seasonings;

- Canned fruits and bottled juices; and

- Frozen meals of all kinds.

The addition of sugar to such foods is bizarre to say the least. After all, what baby needs sugar in their formula, or why does cheese need to be sweetened? The answers are many, but begin with a few simple truths.

One is that we are just plain confused about how our bodies work and what we should be eating for true and optimal health.

The bulk of this book is going to address this particular issue, but also the second reason that sugars are added to foods as well. And that is that the commercial food industry is actually encouraging people to consume the products that commercial farmers grow.

Why Sugar?

Large scale food makers produce foods that are cheap, filling, and capable of being processed into many different forms, including sweeteners. And these sweeteners are the ones we have been cued (some say "trained") to prefer or develop a taste for.

A single illustration of this can be found in the use of corn. In the current era around 55% of all "sweeteners" that are put to use in drinks and foods will be made from corn. This is in addition to the various corn fillers that bulk up foods ranging from sliced meats to pet foods.

This is also why the abundance of soy, corn (used to make corn syrup), and wheat products seem to fill our grocery shelves. Some studies have shown that there are almost no products available without one or more of those three major food crops in their lists of ingredients. And yet, many people are sensitive or allergic to them and these foods may serve no nutritional function into the foods in which they are added. Added sugars are a prime example of this.

Added Sugars are a Growing Problem

In a 2012 article in *US News and World Report*, two journalists made a significant point when they said that the food industry was marketing "bigger, juicier, saltier, sweeter, crunchier…most of all, more." And it is that last word, "more", that seems to be the problem. Almost every manufactured food has more and more processed ingredients, and this is causing many foods to be the same as boxes, bags, and cans of chemicals instead of true food sources.

Adding sugars to many different kinds of foods may create a market for them, but they also force people to develop a taste for ever sweeter (and the same thing goes for added salt making people crave saltier foods) foods and beverages.

As an example, the soft drink known as Coca Cola was once made strictly with cane sugar. Because the modern palette favors foods that are much sweeter, American bottles and cans of this beverage are now made entirely from corn syrup - which has a sweetness factor around 20% greater than table sugar (sucrose).

So, you don't even have to own a sugar bowl to add sugar to the diet every single day. Just drink a single can of soda and you are getting a huge dose of sugar, but if you eat a package of snack crackers, you are probably getting a lot of added sugar as well.

Don't forget that any fruits and vegetables, grains or breads, and even dairy products that you eat will also have *natural* sources of sugar as well. These are the types of sugars that kept people at healthier weights less than a century ago, but which are becoming the lesser consumed types.

All of this sugar consumption adds up (quite literally) in the body, in the form of fat, health problems, and addiction. It can get pretty overwhelming when you realize just how much sugar you are asking your body to process each day, and what it actually means to your health.

Sugar in the Body

Why is sugar so overwhelming? We'll keep this as simple and straightforward as possible, but you do need to understand what happens when you eat sugar.

The entire body needs energy - right down to the tiniest cells. If they don't have energy, they don't work. If our cells stop functioning, our tissues, bodily fluids, and organs cease to operate as well. As an example, for your skin to mend from a simple little scratch it requires energy devoted to making new cells, shedding old ones, and fighting infection at the site of the injury.

You need energy all of the time and from head to toe.

Energy Crisis

This energy comes from the foods we eat. Food is made up of many things. The basic "macronutrients" (which are called macro because we need them in huge quantities) are fat, protein, and carbohydrate. We also have to take water, fiber, vitamins, and minerals from our foods as well.

Our bodies are amazing machines where the digestion and metabolism of food is concerned. Cells understand what to do with each component, where to send it, and how to use it to function properly.

Drink water and it is distributed properly, eat fiber and the body uses it to cleanse the digestive system, consume fat and the body wants to burn it up for energy - unless something else is already being used for that purpose. And that is where sugar becomes a problem.

All foods are, basically, digested in similar ways. We put them in our mouths, chew them (which introduces them to enzymes), swallow them (introducing more enzymes and triggering "metabolites"), and these break the various parts of the food (protein, carbohydrates, fats, waters, etc.) into smaller components that the cells know how to use for energy.

When we eat carbohydrates (and sugar is categorized as a carbohydrate or "carb"), the enzymes will break it down into "glucose". This is then absorbed by the body and allowed to enter into the bloodstream, and is why we often talk about our "blood sugar" levels. If you have ever guzzled a sports drink or glass of juice, you know that glucose can hit the blood stream almost immediately.

The Race to the Cells

Ideally, however, your diet should produce very little changes in blood sugar. Instead, it should keep you at an "even keel" and allow you to feel hunger when food is needed, to feel energized when that is required, and to have enough stored energy to help with any physical challenges that are not too great or overly long.

Endurance athletes, as an example, have to train to run dozens of miles, lift heavy weights, or swim for an hour or more. The average human does not need to concern themselves with the creation of the massive stores of energy and highly developed muscles that endurance demands. Instead, it is best to eat a balanced diet suited to lifestyle.

When we eat such a diet, the macronutrients will not all be put to use by the same metabolic processes, though they can often overlap along some of the "pathways" used to transfer materials to the cells, organs, and tissue. Protein will be put to use in making muscle, hormones, and transporting signals between cells - among other things. Fats and carbs should be used for energy, with fat providing more than half of the body's energy requirement.

Fat always breaks down into fatty acids that the blood recognizes and uses for any cells that require energy. When fat in the diet is not immediately needed for energy, it is put into storage as…you guessed it…fat.

Unfortunately, the size of fat cells is unlimited and we can store as much fat as imaginable. This occurs two ways - as adipose tissue that we see on most parts of the body and as fat that rests atop organs. Neither is very healthy, but it is the unseen fat that causes the greatest risks. And it is always best to simply choose a diet and lifestyle that keeps as little fat on the body as possible.

Carbs, as we know, enter the bloodstream as glucose and is gobbled up by cells that need energy that very moment. This is why our modern, carb heavy diets will prevent us from burning up fat as energy because carbs win the race and get to the cells first.

The undigested glucose that remains after the cells have taken their fill of energy is sent for storage in the liver. Now, the liver is good at distributing this sugar into the body whenever we are low on food - such as when we are sleeping or in between meals. It can also send carbs into storage as fat to prevent wasted energy too.

However, when our bodies are kept low on carbs at all times, the digestive system starts to use fats as energy. It takes it directly from the foods ingested as well as tapping into any stored fat on the body. In other words, if you are low on sugar and simple carbs, the body liquidates fat instead.

Look at it this way: You use a 21 day sugar detox. At the end of the time you have only a tiny reserve of glucose stored in the body. Whenever you eat, the body knows to send all of the energy directly to the cells and put only that tiny leftover bit into storage, which is going to be used up during daily exercise and general activities - including sleeping.

Before that 21 day detox, however, you were carrying a few more pounds of fat because your body was used to sending glucose into your cells for energy and storing most of the fat you ate because it was rarely being used. By turning around the processes, eating more fat and no sugar, you are telling your body that it should always use fat to create energy.

Now, this does not mean that a diet void of carbs is a good one. Remember that carbohydrates are called macronutrients for one main reason - the body needs them.

The Brain and Carbs

This is especially true for the brain. The brain is a
tremendously vital organ and its cells cannot operate on fatty
acids (the acids produced from fat in the diet), but instead
need glucose to function.

While people following low carb diets like to argue that the
body will create "ketones" that provide enough energy to cells
(such as brain cells) that do not metabolize fatty acids, there is
always the need for glucose.

Even if the liver and kidneys are relied upon to create glucose
from available resources in the body, it would require a
tremendous amount of protein to ensure this occurs. And
there is always a risk that the body will have to liquidate
muscle in order to create adequate supplies of glucose for the
brain and other similarly difficult cells.

So, in summary, you must eat all of the macronutrients if you
are to remain as healthy as possible, but you do want to keep
firm control on the quantities and quality of the
macronutrients you consume.

Just knowing that your body prefers to use fat as a form of
energy proves that reducing carbohydrate intake and cutting
out the valueless forms of it - sugar and simple carbs - is going
to improve metabolism. And metabolism is a very important
matter.

Metabolism 101

You need to look at metabolism in two different ways. The
first way is the "technical" one in which the macronutrients
you consume are broken down into the energy you need to
remain alive and functioning.

As we just explained above, the kidneys and liver might be able to "synthesize" some glucose in order to help the brain meet its needs for energy, but this is not a very reliable process because you may not eat enough protein to allow the organs to do this. It proves that the technical processes of metabolism are incredibly complex and work best when they are fed by a very well rounded and complete diet.

Your body metabolizes the food you eat and the fluids you drink and dispenses all of the nutrients into the cells. It is not, however, a perfect system because you control the foods and beverages you put into your body and these may not always be "the best". It is also imperfect because it still operates in an "ancient" way and clashes with a modern diet.

As we explained above, the common choice to indulge in too many simple carbs and sugars means that the body's natural tendency to burn fat is interrupted by a poor dietary choice. Ancient human beings were not big on sugar and simple carbs - in fact, they didn't really encounter them at all. This means that the body has been programmed and designed to metabolize fat for energy but is blunted in its natural pathways by the modern reliance on sugar.

This stops the body from being a good fat burning machine and it also impacts metabolism by preventing nutrients from being distributed properly and by slowing the pace of things to very low levels.

The Metabolic Rate

The second way to look at metabolism is as a sort of "rate" or "pace" at which the body performs the processes described in the technical definition of the term. For example:

How fast does your body use up the energy (or calories) that you ingest?

How fast is the metabolism of other members of your family? After all, around 5% of your metabolic rate has to do with genes.

How much exercise and activity do you do each day?
How muscular is your body? Muscle burns more calories than fat,
so people who are fit tend to have "faster" metabolisms.

All of these things will have an effect on the rate of your metabolism, and one of the things you want to always seek to do is to increase the speed and make your metabolism faster. What do we mean by faster? Generally speaking, if you are going to cut your sugar addiction it will automatically involve taking steps that result in an increase in your body's metabolic rate. This is because you will cease to rely on carbs as a primary source of energy and turn more to fats instead. This will create a scenario in which most of the food you consumed is used by the body immediately - this is a fast metabolism. Slow metabolisms are those that don't need all of the food eaten and send it into storage for later metabolism into the cells. Thus, you are going to carry extra fat because of a slow metabolism.

Developing a faster metabolism means you are going to eat more often than you do now. For example, people who eat every two to three hours are stimulating the metabolism to get to work, and this leads the body into a beneficial pattern. Rather than having a body that is trying to avoid starvation (because you are only eating every five or six hours), the body that eats every two to three is going to feed its muscle and not its fat.

For instance, you skip breakfast almost every day and don't really eat until dinner. This sends an emergency signal to the body that food is in scant supply. Yes, it sounds primitive, but human evolution is still impacting our very modern bodies. So, whenever a meal is skipped it works as a warning sign to the body that some fat storage may be necessary over the next few meals. It also creates a pattern that holds the metabolism at a slower pace to ensure that the body is not using up all of its energy. In other words, your body is not burning calories very quickly at all.

This problem or pattern is reinforced if you skip meals or eat lightly all day and then stuff yourself at dinner. Sure, the total calorie load for the day is relatively low, but you just ate them all at once. This tells the body that you may not have ongoing access to food and it begins packing away fat to help you through the issue.

If, however, you tell the body that food supplies are not a concern, it will just feed the muscles and skip the whole fat storage thing. And this is particularly true if you are eating all of the "right" things every two to three hours.

Eating Right is a Major Key

"Sorry, there's no magic bullet. You gotta eat healthy and live healthy to be healthy and look healthy. End of story."
— Morgan Spurlock, Don't Eat This Book: Fast Food and the Supersizing of America

By that we mean that you are eating miniature and complete meals that feature a lot of fiber, fat, and protein.

For example, a small salad with chopped egg or chicken is a great example of an ideal meal.

You want to consider how your body metabolizes the foods you eat; and consuming protein (which takes twice as many calories to digest as carb or fat) and fiber is putting your body's metabolism to work, giving it loads of nutrients, and telling it that fat storage is not needed. It also helps you feel satiated while keeping blood sugar completely under control. Yes, we are back at blood sugar. This is because we cannot get too far from or avoid this major issue.

If we accept that nutrition is a major component of a faster metabolism, and that sugar is nutritionally void, we can see that sugar is no good for our metabolic processes. Nutrients are meant to give us the materials that our bodies cannot make on their own, and well chosen foods are great for helping us with this need. However, sugar and many of the simple carbs do not work in this way, and so they should not figure prominently (or appear at all) in the diet.

If our diets were ideally suited to the modern diet or the SAD, the body would be able to use up glucose right away to give the energy needed for motion, activity, and basic functions. However, this is not the case. Modern people don't usually eat optimized diets, and so the body is forced to take that energy (glucose) and store it in the cells for later use.

The Function of Insulin

To trigger this storage process the body has to create insulin. If the body cannot make enough insulin, the sugar stays in the blood stream and causes a lot of damage. This is most commonly seen in the disease known as diabetes, and why injections or doses of insulin are required to keep it under control.

So, when we eat carbs, the body breaks them down into glucose, and this is released into the bloodstream through the digestive tract. The body then makes insulin to tell the different cells to use the glucose, and this allows the blood sugar to decrease. This, in turn, tells the body to stop making insulin, and this slows down the amount of glucose going into the cells.

What that paragraph describes is a rise and fall in blood sugar, which we all experience many times per day. It is why we get hungry, tired, energized, etc. It is also a relatively delicate balancing act that is made more difficult by the consumption of simple carbs that are so close to glucose that the cells cannot use them properly.

Simple Carbohydrates

Here is what we mean:

You eat a donut that is chock full of sugar, fats, and carbs. This donut has around 300 calories meant to provide the body with energy. However, these calories have very little actual nutrition - such as vitamins, minerals, or even fiber to help with digestion. So, you eat this donut (and you probably drink coffee, milk, or juice with it too), and this introduces simple carbs to the body. These are carbs that are so close to pure sugar that the body doesn't have to do much to process them.

They are also frequently called "empty" calories because they give the body the "potential" for creating energy, but do not provide much in the way of actual nutrition.

With both nutritious and empty calories, the body releases a flow of insulin to tell the cells to use this sugar as energy. However, you are not likely to need that many calories-worth of energy at a single instant (remember, we are talking about a 300 calorie donut). Just consider that you are not often jogging or doing a lot of physical work as you eat a donut with coffee. So, your body now sends that glucose into storage - as fat. Also, it is unlikely that your digestive system is going to remain satisfied for very long because of the lack of nutrients and fiber in this sort of "meal", and you are going to be hungry again in a very short period of time.

The Major Problems

This tells us that frequent meals made up of simple carbs will cause you to:

- Experience highs and lows in blood sugar;
- Boost insulin creation and fat storage; and
- Feel the need to eat more often - and to crave more sugar.

Sadly, the story doesn't end here because simple carbs are also void of nutrients too. They are actually known to decrease the level of nutrient in the body because they require the use of nutrients and minerals to be fully digested.

After all, that bag of white sugar, bottle of soda, or piece of hard candy are all made from refined sugar. This is a substance that has been entirely depleted of protein, minerals or vitamins. It has nothing needed for metabolism and digestion, and that means that it "takes" without giving anything in return, creating a negative result.

They also are known for their "free radical" content that can lead to inflammation and cellular damage in the body. This is why sugar is known for causing a lot of wear and tear on many organs and leading to physical signs often associated with aging or even with drug use.

Sugar is not dealt with properly in the body, it tends to result in "incomplete" carbohydrate metabolism that can leave behind materials that the body is unable to manage. Just consider:

- One of the materials created by the breaking down of glucose is pryuvate or pyruvic acid. This accumulates in the brain and the red blood cells. Because pyruvic acid is a metabolite, it can actually impair cells from getting enough oxygen and functioning as needed. Red blood cells appear in all organs, and when cells within organs die because of this metabolic problem it is usually a sign that degenerative disease of the organ or system will begin.

- We mentioned "acid" above. It has to be pointed out that the consumption of sugar makes the body an overly acidic place. This has one immediate and harmful impact - loss of bone density. Whenever the body is out of balance in this way, it pulls calcium from any available source including the teeth and the bones.

- We know that leftover glucose ends up in the liver in the form of glycogen. We also know that there is a limit to how much of this the liver will safely retain. When your daily diet has a lot of sugar and simple carbs converted to glucose, it can make the liver expand and begin shedding the glycogen. It turns them into fatty acids that are sent into storage in any available fat. This adds to the fat cells and is the most basic explanation of how your pants might get tighter and your belly a bit bigger when you eat a sugary and high carb diet.
- Fat doesn't just appear in visible places (as we mentioned earlier). When the fat cells have accepted all of the fatty acids possible, the blood takes the remaining fat and delivers it to storage areas on top of major organs. This forces such vital organs as the liver, heart, and kidneys to slow down and perform badly. When organs are under strain from fat, it negatively impacts all other bodily systems. Circulation is poor, lymphatic channels do not drain properly, swelling increases due to blood pooling, red blood cells lose their quality while white blood cells increase in number and tissue creation declines.
- Production of cortisol increases due to high insulin production. This happens when we eat too much sugar and too little nutrient. The body releases insulin to request that cells accept the sugar from the bloodstream. The process by which the brain is told

that blood sugar has stabilized is not as fast as it could be, and this often allows the body to make too much insulin and to create a condition known as hyperglycemia.

This creates a craving for sweets in order to help boost the blood sugar back up to a safe level. The issue also puts the body and the brain in serious danger, and this cues the release of cortisol, which is a stress hormone. Cortisol communicates with the liver and tells it that an emergency is occurring and that stored glycogen has to be released to counteract the rapid decline in blood sugar. However, most people have already eaten sweet foods to counteract the problem, and so there is yet another surge of blood sugar. This, clearly, creates an ongoing problem that is almost impossible to stop unless sugar and simple carbs are eliminated.

- Cortisol production is a difficult task for the body's adrenal glands, and this can unbalance the entire hormonal system altogether. And this can lead to a long list of ongoing health problems ranging from depression and allergies to degenerative diseases and obesity.

Yes, that daily candy bar, can or two of soda, or spoonful of sweetener in your coffee could feasibly be wreaking havoc throughout your entire body.

In our discussion about fructose and glycemic index in the next chapter, we'll look even more at the science behind sugar's ability to make us look older, fatigued, and generally unwell. For now, it is simply important to understand that it does have such powers over our bodies.

Of course, all of this should come as no surprise because human beings are not really meant to eat diets high in processed and refined foods. Everything from sugar and white flour to trans fats and even certain starchy vegetables were not really part of the human diet over the millions of years of human evolution.

Our bodies are not meant to consume these processed foods, and so they cause a lot of troubles when we do eat them. Even such "healthy" foods as whole grains were not part of Paleolithic humans' diets, and this is why we see so many food related allergies and diseases.

Hidden Sugar

Can you benefit from simply cutting out all white sugar? Yes, but you have to know about the hidden sugars in other simple carb foods too. These include:

- Starchy foods that are simple carbs such as white potatoes, white rice, white flour, bread, pretzels, crackers, pasta, bagels, etc.
- "Natural" sugars such as brown sugar, honey, sugar cane juice, raw cane sugar, and the different nectars (such as agave) that are being touted as good alternatives.
- The different syrups such as maple, brown rice, high fructose, malt, etc.

- Molasses
- Chemically created sugars such as dextrose, sucrose, and fructose.
- Lactose from dairy products such as yogurt, cream cheese, and some packaged cheese.

Now, that list might really feel a bit overwhelming. After all, you might wonder, will I ever be able to eat something like a cheese sandwich or a bowl of cereal again? The answer is a most definite yes, but it is also that you probably won't find such foods all that appealing once you break a sugar addiction.

The Solution

Sugar is an addiction. The human body does not need refined sugar, and certainly does not benefit from eating it on a daily basis. While the body and brain require "carbohydrates", this is not ever going to mean the same thing as refined white sugar, or too many simple carbs.

Carbohydrates give the body a way to create energy, but choosing a steady diet of nutritionally void carbs is going to make you gain weight, suffer from all kinds of health problems, and live in a way that is a bit out of control (much the same as many drug addicts).

Instead, a human body benefits from the fiber and nutrient rich ways that sugar might enter the blood stream - such as when ingested in various fruits and vegetables or high quality protein or dairy. We don't ever need those "sugar loads" that we constantly dump into our blood streams.

The reason that modern humans are plagued by diseases such as high blood pressure, diabetes, obesity, and strokes or heart attacks tends to begin with diet. If most people would go on a sugar detox it would make for a lot of positive changes in terms of health care.

For example, rather than eating a cookie or two (or five) each day, it is far better for the body to consume a high protein food such as a single hard-boiled egg or a slice of chicken. This doesn't affect the blood sugar though it allows the body to create all kinds of energy.

Additionally, when we consume complex carbohydrates such as those in vegetables, fruits, and most high fiber foods, we create a "long, slow burn" of energy that reduces hunger, converts cells into little fat burning machines, and generally allows us to remain free of common health complaints.

So, the solution we propose is a sugar detox diet that is carefully planned to eliminate every single source of unneeded sugar. We are going to suggest a 21 day diet as this is the typical length of time to destroy the drug like "pathways" and regulation that a life of sugar eating creates. It is also a scientifically suggested length of time to create or alter any specific habit, and sugar is most certainly a habit.

Twenty-One Days and Done

Yes, in three short weeks you can overcome a lifetime of bad dietary habits, but we won't lie and say it is easy.

This is because sugar does indeed act just like a drug in the brain. Studies have shown a few very relevant facts. These are:

- We are always told that sweets and sugary foods are "bad", and because of this, many people follow a trend of avoiding sugar and junk food and then binging on large amounts of it. This is the same behavior that drug abusers follow, and when it applies to sugar consumption, it creates certain hormonal reactions in the brain that are similar to commonly abused drugs.

- Sugar causes people to behave in an agitated manner or to experience withdrawal when it is totally eliminated from the diet.
- Chronic periods of sugar binging cause hormonal responses in the body and the brain. Sugar energy hits the brain cells at all levels, and this means that each time you binge on sugar it impacts the brain. Studies have shown that lab animals given the same sort of sugar laden diets of sugar addicts experience brain behaviors similar to people struggling with drug use.
- Sugar appears in many ways, and even a meal with white potatoes can trigger a bad reaction, just like a small exposure to a difficult drug.
- Sugar sensitization occurs in those who eat a lot of it. This means that their bodies continually absorb more and more of it, without creating the same response. Thus, sugar is a drug because it allows someone to need more and more to get the same reaction.
- Studies show that the pleasure factor of sugar causes most creatures (humans and lab animals) to eat around six times the amount of food needed.

This tells us that it is imperative to begin cutting out all of the unnecessary forms of sugar. We can get more than enough "sweetness" from an all natural diet, and it just takes a few weeks of hard work to cut the addiction.

Not only will we cease to harm our bodies at the cellular level when we bring our sugar consumption to an end, but we will get our diets under control, our appetite will become natural rather than artificial, and anyone following this simple program will shed up to five pounds in the first week and then more weight each week thereafter.

Will it be easy? No, but it will be well worth it. This is because most people who cut their sugar addiction will look better, feel better, sleep better, reduce a lot of the symptoms of illness or disease caused by sugar and simple carb consumption, and generally help their bodies to begin functioning at optimal levels.

Let's take a look at a sugar detox diet to see just how simple it is to cut out sugar and begin to repair our bodies from the cells out!

Warning: In case you experience any physical or mental health problems like anxiety, depression, or other drastic mood changes while eliminating sugar from your life, please see a doctor.

Chapter Two

A Sugar Detox Diet

"Just because you're not sick doesn't mean you're healthy" ~Author Unknown

By now, you should have a fairly good idea of why sugar can and should be cut from the diet. You can get plenty of all natural energy (glucose) without eating anything that has been processed. Sugar triggers drug like activities in the brain, prevents your "satiety" factor to tell you that you are overdoing it and/or are "full", and keeps you on a roller coaster in which you "crash" as insulin puts sugar into storage and then makes you hungry again very soon afterward. Clearly, there is so much wrong with sugar that it becomes a mystery as to why we haven't made a point of cutting it out of our diets sooner. However, there is the commercial factor to consider. A bit later on we are going to look at some conspiracy theory-like issues connected to sugar in processed foods, and even why women might be more prone to sugar addiction than some men.

For now, we just need to remember that sugar is no one's friend. In fact, the human body has been designed to burn fat rather than sugar as a form of energy, and yet fat tends to have a much worse reputation than sugar or simple carbs.

Why? It can be linked to those conspiracy theories we'll discuss a bit later, but it also has to do with simple misunderstandings and misinformation. Because we don't want to "be fat", many of us assume we shouldn't eat it. This is, actually, backwards thinking!

For instance, we've almost all heard about diets such as the globally famous Atkins and South Beach diets. These are two ways of eating that require you to cut carbs to extreme levels and emphasize healthy fats

Diets of this kind might limit specific food groups - such as vegetables that are on the starchy side, and even ask that you forgo things like bread, grain, and potatoes during a one or two week period. Again, this is to help the body detox, but some of these plans are a bit off the mark.

For instance, they allow people to eat dangerously high amounts of "saturated" fat, and that is never advisable as it can clog arteries and create unhealthy amounts of cholesterol in the blood stream. It is only with a balanced approach to eating that you can cut your sugar habits and remain in the peak of health.

While it is entirely true that the body uses fat far more efficiently than it does sugar (when it is for creating energy it normally gives twice the amount of energy that sugar carbs will), it still has to be a "safer" fat.

This usually means a monounsaturated variety, with only limited amounts of polyunsaturated and saturated allowed. For example, avocados and nuts are often said to be fattening because they do have a high amount of it, but they both contain only small amounts of saturated fat. They are nutrient dense foods with a lot to offer and are much better for you than some whole wheat bread or a cup of artificially sweetened yogurt.

Confusing right? Let's take a few moments more to assess this issue.

Optimal Energy

Consider that human evolution occurred over a period of time during which hunter/gatherers became farmers. Because food was always an issue for the hunter and gatherer, their bodies began to evolve storage systems for any calories that they did not use. When the body did need energy, it could burn up that little bit of fat as needed. They could also exist off of a huge variety of different foods - which is rare in the animal kingdom.

For example, one day a human being might ingest a huge quantity of meat from a freshly killed animal, but the next day they might be able to forage only a huge number of berries and leaves. The human body is capable of synthesizing most of what it needs from a diet as diverse as this, and this is a major benefit for modern eaters too.

Modern humans don't need to store any substantial amounts of fat because we are rarely living as hunter/gatherers any longer. Instead, we should be eating fat as a major energy source because it is put to use in the body almost as soon as it is eaten. It is not processed in the same ways that carbs are, and modern people have made the grievous error of conditioning their bodies to burn sugar rather than relying on fat.

Smarter diets, similar to those we just mentioned above are actually designed to start reprogramming the body to use fat for energy, but some grossly overlook the hazards of eating too much saturated fat and cholesterol, and cutting out the nutrients and fiber from fruits and vegetables. The sugar detox approach is less rigid and encourages you to eat a diet that is natural, balanced, and which features complex carbs and fiber.

A Good Example

To better understand an optimal diet, it helps to think of the body like a car that needs diesel fuel to run, but for which there is only rocket fuel available. Now, that little car can realistically burn up the rocket fuel to operate, but it would eventually damage a lot of the different parts and systems doing so.

Your body is being damaged by every spoonful of sugar or simple carb that you eat because it is creating a type of fuel that, while useable, is not ideally suited as a primary source of energy.

Sugars and simple carbs will burn up fast and create "wasted" energy that has to be put somewhere, and it is turned into…you guessed it…fat.

Just stop to consider what our bodies store - they store fat. This is because it is the ideal material for the body to use as energy. If sugar was the ideal fuel, the body would be designed to store a lot of sugar, but it doesn't.

This means that a sugar detox diet is going to help you to convert your body back into a fat burning system rather than one that is being constantly conditioned to deal with sugar. However, it is not all that easy to do this.

It requires you to begin retraining yourself, and this often means you will have to re-learn how to eat. Earlier in this book we mentioned the typical breakfast of OJ and a bagel. The first three to five days that you don't eat this, it is going to feel very odd. That big glass of orange sweetness and that huge load of carbs from the bagel are going to be sorely missed.

However, by the fifth to seventh day of burning up fat for energy, you are going to feel a bit sick thinking about guzzling a glass of sugary juice. Instead, you will actually crave the egg white omelet full of spinach and mushrooms or the handful of almonds and the cup of plain Greek yogurt. Why? You will have cured yourself of the sugar habit/addiction and started feeling all of the amazing benefits.

A Day in the Life

So, what exactly does a day on a sugar detox diet look like? Well, a good "starter" menu would look like this:
- Breakfast:
    o 1/2 cup plain oatmeal (not instant)
    o 1 tbsp flax seed
    o 3 egg whites
- Snack:
    o 1 tbsp unsweetened, all natural peanut butter
    o 1 apple
- Lunch:
    o 4 oz grilled chicken breast
    o 2 cups mixed salad vegetables - include greens, peppers, and cucumbers
    o Splash of balsamic vinegar as dressing
    o 1/2 sweet potato
- Snack
    o 1 cup raw veggies
    o 4 tbsp homemade hummus
- Dinner:

- o 4 oz broiled salmon
- o 1 cup green vegetables (raw or cooked)
- o 2 cups mixed salad veggies - including greens
- o Splash of balsamic to dress salad
- o 1/2 sweet potato
- Late night snack:
  - o 1/4 (around 15) almonds
- At least 8 glasses of water (from 6-8 ounces each) and some green tea for energy

You can see that there are plenty of carbs on this plan, it is simply that they come in the form of fresh vegetables, fruits, fats, and protein.

In fact, this single day shows the sort of "pyramid" that most people will begin to follow as they shift from a heavily laden carbohydrate-rich diet to one that is meant to burn fat for energy and eliminate cravings for sugar.

The pyramid we describe would feature healthy fats as the largest portion of the diet, lean proteins as the next level, non-starchy vegetables after that, a small amount of allowable carbs (complex from fruit or some grains), and little to no sugar.

What would happen when you started eating like that? That is what we now consider...

What to Expect

First of all, the diet is called a "detox" for very obvious reasons - you are detoxifying the body. And just like all other types of detox, you will face some serious challenges. These include:

- Headache

- Irritability (some people experience substantial and relatively "wild" irritability)
- Cravings
- Body aches
- Congestion
- Sluggishness and low energy
- Hazy thinking
- High emotional states
- Skin changes (remember, your body is adjusting and releasing toxins which can cause rashes, acne, and irritation)
- Dizziness
- Interest in foods that supply simple carbs (for example, you may always be a cookie and cake eater and yet find yourself suddenly craving a lot of potatoes and bread - this is a form of addiction transference and is a sign that your body already knows where to get a sugar fix if needed).
- Dehydration
- Cold and flu like symptoms
- Bloating or gas
- Body odor and bad breath
- Disrupted sleep patterns
- Strange thoughts

The good news is that a lot of people who do this diet will often agree that by the fourth or fifth day of remaining free of sugar they are feeling much stronger. After two weeks a lot of people are confident that they have this particular issue "kicked", and after three weeks, most people feel so much better that they don't even go for the "celebratory" sugar options.

In other words, of all of the negatives listed above, few will remain by day four or five. So, ask yourself if optimal health is worth enduring three to five days of problems? Yes…it is!

"I never touch sugar, cheese, bread...
I only like what I'm allowed to like. I'm beyond temptation. There is no weakness. When I see tons of food in the studio, for us and for everybody, for me it's as if this stuff was made out of plastic. The idea doesn't even enter my mind that a human being could put that into their mouth. I'm like the animals in the forest. They don't touch what they cannot eat."
— Karl Lagerfeld

How Much Sugar is Okay?

However, we did just use the term celebratory sugar. Most anti-sugar advocates indicate that you can eat sugar as a "treat" or during times of celebration. However, there are two issues here:

1. You may no longer feel that sugar is right for you or your body. It may manifest as absolutely no interest in the consumption of sugar and simple carbs. In other words, you are no longer tempted to eat these things; or

2. You may worry that once the floodgates are opened and you eat that piece of cake or enormous brownie that it is "all downhill" from there.

Interestingly enough, both theories have a lot of truth to them. For example, people who go completely sugar free (even avoiding sugar substitutes) will remove items such as ketchup, breads, and most cereals from their food lists. They might do so because they know that these are highly tempting foods, or they might eliminate them because they understand that they have completely lost their "taste" for them.

Consider that some people will go sugar free for the recommended 21 day period and then take a sip of juice or a bit of candy and discover that it is now sickeningly sweet to them. Others might take that sip or nibble and feel the urge to consume enormous quantities of this food (drug).

So, there is no set figure or amount of sugar that we can tell you is "okay" for you to consume. This is a very personal issue, but the one word of advice that we would give repeatedly is that the less sugar you allow in the diet the better, and cutting it altogether is fantastic.

You could also follow the recommendations of the World Health Organization that says that you should "eat no more than 10% of the daily BMR from added sugar sources".

Note that they say "added" sugar, and this means things like honey or table sugar rather than from the fructose or glucose in fruits and vegetables, etc.

This statement by the WHO might also make many ask what the "BMR" is, and the answer is that it is the acronym for your "basal metabolic rate". Again, we are going to have to consider metabolism in order to understand how harmful sugar is to the body.

BMR is Useful

Every person has a baseline of calories that they need to keep their body functioning. This baseline does not include any allowances for exercise or physical activity. Instead, it is the lowest number of calories you could consume to maintain your current weight and still function fully. In other words, it is the amount of energy your body needs to keep all of the organs, systems, and cells operating.

It is a relatively general number because it doesn't consider if you are a person who runs ten miles every day or someone who sits on the sofa for hours on end. It uses some basic math, and the formulas are different for men and women (though they both use age, height, and weight). They are:

- Adult female: 655 + (4.3 x weight in lbs.) + (4.7 x height in inches) - (4.7 x age in years); or

- Adult male: 66 + (6.3 x body weight in lbs.) + (12.9 x height in inches) - (6.8 x age in years).

You just plug in the figures that are appropriate for your body and get that basic number of calories.

Then, if you want to follow the advice of the WHO, you calculate what ten percent of those calories would mean. Let's say you find you should be eating around 1575 calories each day to maintain your weight. The WHO says it should be okay for you to eat around 150-160 calories in the form of added sugar.

Now, this is a discretionary provision, and a lot of dietary recommendations provide only that small figure for total daily discretionary calories. What we mean is that many health and nutrition experts would say that 150 to 200 calories per day can be allotted to things like sugar and fat *combined*. So, you might opt for a less lean meat for dinner and see all of the extra calories lost to that fattier protein instead of a sugary sweet.

Of course, this immediately tells us exactly why so many people using a sugar detox see such substantial amounts of weight loss during the first week or so. They may be people who unwittingly consume hundreds of empty calories each day by consuming a lot more than the recommended levels of added sugar. Once they cut the source of the calories, they start shedding pounds. Additionally, they are using fat for energy, and that means that they are optimizing their metabolisms.

What we recommend is that you calculate your BMR and then use the WHO allowance to determine how many grams of sugar you could feasibly add to the diet each day to remain within the recommended allowance. This too involves only the simplest mathematics because you need only divide the number of calories by four.

Why four? This is because sugar has four calories per gram. Of course, this might make you wonder why we are even discussing the issue. After all, we are actually dealing with a sugar detox; a complete removal of sugar from the diet altogether.

Say NO to Added Sugar

The reason we are going over this issue is because it can be incredibly enlightening to discover how much sugar is considered "safe" to consume each day, and yet how much added sugar is in most packaged and prepared foods.

For example, a jar of spaghetti sauce can have 12 or more grams of sugar per serving. A serving size might be 1/2 cup, and most people easily consume a cup or more at a meal. This means that you could be eating 24 grams of sugar with that plate of simple carb-laden pasta. Enjoy a carton of fat free chocolate milk at breakfast that same day and you just swallowed 54 grams of sugar in one fell swoop. That would mean that with just two dietary choices you ate almost twice the added sugar that would be considered "healthy", and yet you didn't even get a piece of candy or a scoop of ice cream out of the deal!

Eating in this way is not uncommon, and even if you did the recommended 30 minutes of exercise it might not be sufficient to provide any sort of weight regulation or weight loss.

This is only one of the reasons that we insist a *total* sugar detox is necessary. And the only way to be absolutely certain that you are not accidentally ingesting a lot of hidden sugars is to avoid pre-packaged, processed, and artificially enhanced foods.

We also suggest that you become an avid label reader if you are going to rely on a few packaged foods. This is because labels are often a good way to find when sugars are being cunningly concealed in a food.

We already provided that list of typical sugars, but let's look again:

- Brown sugar

- Cane sugar

- Corn syrup

- Dextrose

- High fructose corn syrup (HFCS)

- Honey

- Maltodextrin

- Molasses

- Raw sugar
- Turbinado

However, you must also understand that these are not the only types to consider. A label might have terms such as:

- Agave nectar or syrup
- All natural evaporated can juice
- Barley malt
- Beet syrup
- Brown rice syrup
- Coconut syrup
- Dextran
- Fructose
- Golden syrup
- Isomalt
- Maltodextrin
- Organic sucanat
- Raffinose
- Sorbitol
- Sorghum
- And up to 250+ other possible names or terms

For example, you pick up a product and see that it has 25 grams of sugar per serving. That is 100 calories, and yet you may not yet know how much of that is added sugar as opposed to a naturally formed source of sugar such as carbohydrate.

This requires that you read the ingredients. If any sort of added sugar is in the first three ingredients, you don't want to eat it. That is because ingredients are labeled in order of volume or weight. If you see something like turbinado sugar or corn syrup within the first three terms, it is not a good option. In fact, if you see that anything has any more than 2.5 grams of added sugar per every 100 calories, you don't want it in the house or pantry.

Again, however, these are foods that are not allowed during detox, but are going to become acceptable in the post detox period. You may not want such foods at all, but if you need a bit of incentive to keep moving forward through the detox, it can be helpful to know what you will be allowed to eat once you have finished the process.

These allowable cheats are just that - cheats. They are not things that can be eaten every day or in great quantities. They are, as we said earlier, "celebratory" sugars. The piece of cake at the party, the glass of lemonade at the office, etc. - but keep in mind that you might only be able to tolerate a sip of that drink or a fork full of that cake once you are free of sugar. It may be unappealing to your palette - or it may light up a warning light in your brain that you should go no farther! You have to learn your reactions and gauge the impact sugar has on you.

Also, remember that the simple carbs should be seen on the same level as the added sugar. Look at the pile of spaghetti, the chunk of farmer's market bread, or the enormous baked potato as the equivalent of a bowl full of sugar. These foods will do almost all of the same things as eating added sugars when you choose them for your diet, and you need to restrict them quite heavily for the detox, and afterward.

So, to help you get yourself ready for a true sugar detox, and to completely overcome a sugar addiction, you should take the time to learn what foods are allowable.

Allowed Foods

Though this is an extensive list of foods, you still need to take even further considerations when you purchase them. These are:

- We suggest you invest in as many organic fruits, vegetables, meats, dairy, and grains as possible. This ensures that they give your body the ultimate number of nutrients and cut risks of any harmful side effects that might come from pesticides, GMO, and all of the other modern commercial food methodologies.

- We also suggest that you stop and think of substitute foods that might help you with any major cravings. For example, keeping a food journal in the days or weeks ahead of the detox will reveal your most common food choices to you. When you discover that you have a tendency to use things like bottled dressings or sweetened sauces, it will be a wise idea to find substitutions that will encourage your detox process rather than make it more challenging.

  For instance, balsamic vinegar or olive oil and a splash of lemon juice are just fine when salad dressings are needed.

- Plan for protein in every single meal. If you are feeling hungry on the detox, always reach for a lean protein to get you past hurtles.

- No alcohol at all!

- Create a full plan for meals in order to eliminate any problems with cravings or moments when you want something to eat but nothing is pre-made.

Something that a lot of people using the sugar detox claim is that they get super creative with their food choices when using an approved list of foods. So, put on your thinking cap and consider how you will use the following food items

- Apples
- Apricots
- Artichokes
- Avocado
- Bacon
- Bacon
- Balsamic vinegar
- Beans of all kinds
- Beef jerky
- Beets (only one cup per day)
- Bell Peppers
- Berries
- Broccoli
- Brussels sprouts
- Butter
- Cabbage
- Celery
- Canadian bacon
- Canned meats and fish

- Carrots
- Cauliflower
- Cherries
- Citrus fruits of any kind
- Coconut butter
- Coconut flakes
- Coconut oil
- Cucumbers
- Dairy - go for full fat to keep sugar content low
- Eggplant
- Eggs
- Fish and shellfish of all kinds
- Ginger
- Green beans
- Ground lamb, pork, veal, beef, bison
- Herbs
- Kiwi
- Lamb roast
- Lemons
- Lentils
- Limes
- Melons (except watermelon)
- Mushrooms
- Mustard (no sodium)
- Natural, sugar free nut butters

- Nuts
- Olive oil
- Olives
- Onions of all kinds
- Pears
- Peas
- Pumpkin
- Salad greens
- Sauerkraut
- Seeds
- Short ribs
- Spices of all kinds
- Spinach and greens
- Squash
- Steel cut oats
- Tomatoes
- Whole chicken
- Zucchini and summer squash

In addition to these items, you may need to consider if low glycemic foods or foods with natural fructose are a good option for your goals. This is something that needs to be taken seriously if you think that you will struggle too intensely over the course of 21 days. Many people really cannot remain happy without a bit of fruit or natural sugar, and so we suggest you spend some time learning about fructose and the glycemic index, and how to use some smarter food choices to satisfy urges without also sabotaging your plans for a sugar detox.

This is what we consider in the next chapter.

"Well, if it can be thought, it can be done, a problem can be overcome"
— E.A. Bucchianeri, Brushstrokes of a Gadfly

Chapter Three

Overcoming the Challenges

Eating is a natural way to feel happy. Overeating isn't.
-Dr. Deepak Chopra (Author of WHAT ARE YOU HUNGRY FOR?)

Among the worst of the issues associated with a sugar detox diet or just cutting all sources of sugar from your diet are the cravings that come with such a decision. Though you may believe that you feel grumpy or irritable because of some sort of chemical change in the body, a great deal of the emotional turmoil is because you are living with an unmet and irresolvable craving.
You know that you cannot eat the candy, cake, pasta, or high and simple carb food that you desire. It just makes you grumpy.
However, once you get past the detox phase, you can consider adding small amounts of sugar back into your life - though we really don't recommend this as a daily option but as a single celebratory treat every once in a great while.
Here's the thing: We can promise most readers that after 21 days without any sort of sugar (even that found in fruits if you decide to cut them out for the entire period too), the palette won't respond the same ways to many of your once favorite foods.

An Encouraging Tale

"Mary" was an avid junk food fanatic. Each day included the consumption of sweetened beverages such as soda and bottles of iced tea. Each meal was full of white breads, pastas, and starches. She rarely ate any whole foods such as fresh fruits and vegetables, and her fats of choice came out of a deep fryer.

When she was warned that she was showing signs of developing diabetes, she decided to take action. She learned about sugar detox plans and determined that going "cold turkey" for 21 days was the only way to break her addiction to "ring dings", "Twinkies", and all of the rest.

She did not even put a single cherry or slice of apple in her mouth until that 21 day period had passed. And when it was all over and done, she no longer dreamt of eating sweets and mountains of pasta.

Instead, when she was allowed to have a mouthful of her favorite sugary soda, it made her feel queasy. As she tasted her once favorite commercial pastry, she immediately spit it out. Everything tasted chemically sweetened and totally artificial. Her palate had adjusted to a much more natural and flavorful diet.

This is not science fiction or fantasy. This is what happens when we give the body a chance to work in the way it should. When we reject all of the modern commercial food programming, we are often shocked by the delicious flavors that natural food sources provide.

Things we once thought "bland" such as plain yogurt, roasted chicken, or broccoli are suddenly extremely palatable. The fat in the yogurt is like a heavenly and creamy dream and the strong flavor of the vegetable and meat - especially if splashed with a drizzle of high quality olive oil and a bit of fresh lemon juice - are wonderful and satisfying.

Yes, you will be cutting out the salt and artificial flavorings as you do a sugar detox, but you are also showing your body and brain how good it feels to get the best source of energy into each and every cell. The energy that comes mostly from healthy fat and lean protein and limited carbs will give you the clearest head and the "cleanest" energy you have ever experienced.

The one hurtle, however, is getting past that 21 day detox period. And some people do this by allowing themselves a bit of natural sugar. This is why we have to consider the issue of fructose.

Fructose

Before you get very excited thinking that we are suggesting you consume a lot of fructose when experiencing a sugar craving - guess again. Most experts indicate that you can ingest *some* fructose, but only if you understand that *glucose* is the only sugar that the body recognizes as a natural source of energy.

Glucose is the one type of energy or sugar that all life forms can recognize and use. In the human body it is metabolized by multiple organs, meaning that there is no undo load put upon any single part of the body.

This means that there are not many risks to your health whenever you introduce glucose. At least there are no risks when you introduce only small amounts via natural sources (such as the carbohydrates that come from fruits, vegetables, proteins, some dairy, and complex carbs in moderation).

Fructose Takes the Lead

About 20% of the glucose you consume will be metabolized by the liver - the rest is handled by the remaining organs and cells of the body. When glucose is metabolized by your liver it is turned into "glycogen" which allows it to be stored in the liver until it is needed.

Your liver can actually store an immense amount of glycogen before any harm comes to the body (we don't recommend this on an ongoing basis), and this is one of the main reasons that endurance athletes and marathoners will ingest a high carb-load on the evening before a big event. Their liver is going to store a lot of glycogen and then release it in the form of energy when they start to become fatigued from their athletic performance.

However, we know that there are other types of sugars, and fructose seems to be the commercial sugar of choice. In fact, this processed sugar tends to make up nearly 25% of most modern daily caloric intake, which is a radical change from even 40 years ago.

One of the reasons that this is the case is because of the introduction of HFCS (high fructose corn syrup). This was invented in 1966 and by the mid-1970s a vast majority of commercial food makers had switched from "table sugar" which is sucrose to the cheaper and far sweeter fructose. Today, it appears on the list of ingredients for almost every packaged or processed food produced. As already indicated, it can appear in baby formula (with some products at 43% corn syrup solids) as well as serving as the primary ingredient in soft drinks and colas, juices, and most snack foods.

Knowing this makes it much easier to understand why the world is in the midst of an obesity epidemic, but it actually gets worse. This is because fructose has some fairly shocking traits and capabilities.

For example, it has a negative effect on the hormone we know as "leptin". This is the "satiety" hormone, or the chemical that tells us we are full. Fructose has a way of switching this hormone "off" and preventing us from recognizing when we are full and should stop eating - especially when we are eating sugar.

Unfortunately, the high amounts of fructose in many popular foods indicates that people are "hooked" on fructose and sweetened foods, and that they are locked into a vicious cycle of craving sugar, consuming too much of it, spiking and then crashing their blood sugar, storing a lot of fat, and still being hungry more often than ever.

Around 1900 the average person consumed fructose only in the form of their fresh fruits and vegetables. The result of which was an average daily intake of fructose around 15 grams. Today, it is not unusual for someone to ingest more than 70 grams each day - plus any other sugars that could include glucose and more.

Fructose and the Liver

This means that people are exposing their bodies to enormous doses of fructose every day, and that is very bad news for the liver.

Why? This is because the metabolism of fructose tends to be handled mostly by the liver. And while a few grams of the stuff each day wouldn't necessarily be harmful, it is the fact that we are (on the whole) eating dozens of grams of it on a daily basis.

The problems with fructose are many, but the issues you must be aware of are these:

- Fructose, as just mentioned, is metabolized mostly by the liver. Because of the flood of it entering the liver when it is eaten in foods such as soda or candy, it is impossible for the liver to process it properly and turn it into a usable form of sugar for the body. It converts the fructose into "tryglycerides".

- You may or may not know that triglycerides are the form in which most fat appears in the body. That fat you despise on your thighs or your belly is made up of triglycerides, and they also appear in your bloodstream.
- People with heart disease often have hypertriglyceridemia - or too many triglycerides floating around in their blood.
- Fructose also interrupts leptin production and function, and this leads to people overeating and gaining weight. This is because leptin tells your brain that you are full and that you should stop eating. This is one of the main reasons that fructose consumption leads to weight gain.
- Consuming fructose is also believed to lead to something known as insulin resistance, which means that the cells in the body refuse to open up to insulin and accept sugar from the bloodstream, and this is known as diabetes.
- Fructose is what is known as a "hepatotoxin" which means it is toxic to the liver and yet is metabolized 100% by the liver. It depletes the liver of phosphates and creates uric acid in the process. This prevents the creation of nitric acid, which is in charge of blood pressure regulation. This means that you can develop

hypertension by consuming too much fructose, in addition to the fact that it has also probably boosted your bad cholesterol thereby increasing blood pressure.

- We already learned that it converts to pyruvate and causes too much fat to be released and held in the bloodstream.
- Fructose has a tendency to create insulin resistance, and this means that it results in damage to the pancreas.
- Fructose can leave people in a chronic state of inflammation due to the irritant properties it has.

In other words, if you look at all of the things that fructose does to the human body; you can sum them up in a few short words: Fructose ruins the healthy metabolism.
When you eat a lot of fructose you are creating a perpetual cycle of fat production that is almost impossible to break without just eliminating all sources of fructose from the diet.

Fruit Eaters Take Heed

However, we are discussing this issue because we understand that many people struggle desperately with the elimination of all sources of sweetness in their diet. After all, a lifetime of sugar overload is very hard to bring to a sudden halt. And this is why a lot of people doing a sugar detox reassure themselves by saying: "Well, I can eat a lot of fruit instead."
The problem here is that you can't.

Fruit contains fructose, and though it is not a tremendous amount, it is still there. On the "up" side, the fructose you consume in natural fruit sources is accompanied by a lot of fiber and nutrients too. So, we are suggesting that you make an allowance for yourself for a bit of fruit, but to understand how many grams of fructose you are ingesting with each serving.

Earlier in this book we indicated that the WHO put a daily intake of glucose at 10% of the BMR. We would estimate that puts the range from around 12 to 20 grams per day maximum. Now, that is glucose and not just fructose. So, if you are going to rely on a bit of fruit to get you through the 21 day cycle, understand that it will be a very small bit of fruit.

Look at the following table to understand what we mean:

Fruit	Serving	Grams per Serving
Berries	1 cup	7.4
Apple	1 small	9.5
Watermelon (not recommended)	1 cup cubes	11.5
Cherries	1 cup, pitted	4
Lemon/Limes	1 small	Less than one gram
Orange	1 small	6
Strawberries	1 cup	3.8
Kiwi	1 large	4
Melon	1 cup	2.8

Dried fruit (not recommended)	1/4 cup	13
Banana	1 medium, peeled	7
Peach	1 medium	6

So, that handful of berries that you eat at lunch time might push you into a dangerous zone if you elect to have some oats for breakfast and then eat properly the rest of the day. Be careful and be aware of the amount of fruit you choose to eat each day. It is not meant to substitute for any other foods or meals. It can be a wonderful source of nutrition and fiber, but it cannot provide a substantial part of the daily diet.

If you are really feeling challenged by a serious sugar craving, and you fear it is going to push you towards really bad decisions, have at least one or two "fall back" fruits on hand. Seasonally sweet strawberries are ideal because they pack a lot of nutrients, have relatively low fructose content, and are extremely satisfying. In fact, most berries are a good "go to" solution.

Something to remember about fruit, however, is that it does have a relatively high glycemic index, and that is also something you must know about in order to understand the value of your sugar free lifestyle.

Glycemic Index

We've talked a lot about your blood sugar, but we haven't mentioned something that is pretty obvious, and that is that changes in the blood sugar make the body work hard - too hard.

This is often called wear and tear, but it is simply a defense mechanism that your body enacts whenever it discovers that there is sugar in the blood. Of course, we also haven't really gone into any great depth about precisely why the body sounds the "red alert" when sugar enters the blood stream. The simplest answer is that sugar can corrupt and damage cells. It comes about from a process known as glycation of protein. This is when the protein in the blood cells form a bond with the sugar. This forces the cells to change and the proteins will lose their abilities to function properly or remain "elastic".

In other words, glycation is cellular damage, but it is also cellular damage that behaves like a row of carefully aligned dominoes. This is because any cells damaged by the glycation process will also begin to damage the proteins nearby. Hit one protein molecule with glucose and soon its neighbors are showing the same damages. This is most often "seen" in such proteins as elastin and collagen in the skin.

Yes, the most common signs of aging in the skin are loss of elasticity in the collagen and elastin, and this can relate directly to your diet and the amount of glucose you consume. Eat a diet high in sugar and you may have a lot of wrinkles at an early age.

However, glycation is a destructive process for everyone - not just those worried about signs of aging or sagging skin, and one way of reducing all instances of glycation is to go for a diet that is full of low glycemic foods.

These are foods that don't "spike" the blood sugar immediately after consumption, call forth floods of insulin, and do damage. Instead, these are the foods with all natural forms of sugar, lots of fiber, and plenty of protein. Meat, legumes, and veggies are some of the best sources for a low glycemic diet.

How They Work

Do they have any impact on blood sugar? Yes, the low GI foods tend to create a very slow and very moderate increase in the blood sugar over a period of roughly two hours after being eaten. They are not full of carbs that beat fat in the race to supply cells with energy, and so it means that a meal that has a low GI is going to actually push the body to burn up fat rather than relying on glucose.

Remember that we have been continually mentioning the value of foods in terms of their nutrients, fiber, etc. We have also mentioned that most sugary foods create a negative nutrient effect because they consume many nutrients during the digestive and metabolic processes without replacing them or supplying other essential materials. This is why low GI foods are so beneficial - they give a lot of nutrition and they ask the body to use a lot of energy to properly metabolize them.

A bit earlier in this book we spoke about the BMR or the Basal Metabolic Rate. This was the number of calories that your body needs to remain functional, without taking any activity into consideration. There is also the issue known as "thermic effect". This is the number of calories, or the energy, needed to digest the foods consumed.

Many dieting experts like to point out that some foods create a negative calorie balance because they contain nutrients but end up with a zero calorie content (or less) because of the thermic effect. A prime example of this is the trend in "kale chips" that use energy to digest without also bringing in a lot of calories.

So, a low GI diet can be very useful to those seeking to shed weight because it doesn't spike the blood sugar, it creates a long and slow burn of energy, and it can bump up the thermic effect and burn almost the same number of calories as those eaten.

Here is a general breakdown of the thermic effect of popular foods:

- Protein - this is a macronutrient that takes a tremendous number of calories to digest and metabolize - up to 30% of the total calories consumed in many opinions. So, if you eat 350 calories of lean protein, you could reasonably reduce the total caloric intake by up to 30% during the digestion process.

- Carbohydrate - the simple carbs burn almost no energy during digestion and are usually seen as requiring less than 3%of total caloric intake to metabolize. The complex carbs are different and demand a lot of energy. This is because they are often high in fiber, and though the body cannot fully break down insoluble fiber it will keep on trying to do so and burning up calories along the way. Some estimates put this around 10 to 20% of caloric consumption.

- Fat - the body expends very little energy in digesting fat, and this too has a thermic effect of around 3% at the maximum. However, you also already understand that your body recognizes fat as a great source of energy and tends to put it to use immediately if it is not in the running against carbohydrates and sugar.

Using the Information

"The doctor of the future will be oneself."
—Albert Schweitzer

How can you put all of this information to use in your sugar detox plan? It is going to serve you very well to spend time learning about foods that have both the lowest GI levels and that appear on the list of "allowable foods" during detox. These are the foods that will deliver the greatest amount of nutrition and which won't cause any spikes in your blood sugar.

They are also going to be foods that help you to burn the most calories because they tend to have high protein levels and are complex carbs that have a lot of fiber. By challenging the body during digestion, you ensure a long and slow supply of calories. Your blood sugar is kept in check, and you may not produce much blood sugar at all.

A diet that has a low GI (which also means almost no sugar) is known to cut your risks of obesity, heart disease, and diabetes; will give you a lot more energy; will boost the metabolism; will keep your appetite and hunger under control; will encourage weight loss; and will keep your blood sugar at a healthy level.

The glycemic index of any food is stated as a number. It uses glucose as the reference point of 100 and then rates foods based on how they increase blood sugar in comparison. Obviously, the lower the GI number, the better it is as a dietary choice. Anything with a GI more than 55 is going to be considered unsuitable for anyone on a sugar detox diet. Below are the approximate GI values of many popular foods:

Food Source	GI per Serving
Watermelon	103
Potato	93
Rice Cake	91
Pretzels	85
Cornflakes cereal	84
Jelly Beans	80
Donut	76
Waffles	76
White Rice	72
Bagel	72

Wheat Crackers	70
Whole Wheat Bread	69
Honey	58
Pita	57
Banana	56
Brown Rice	55
Oatmeal (instant)	49
Carrots	49
Grapes	46
Spaghetti	43
Apple	38
Beans and Lentils	35

Yogurt	35
Milk (low fat)	32
Milk (whole)	22
Nuts	20
Broccoli	10
Cabbage	10
Lettuce	10
Onions	10
Mushrooms	10
Peppers	10
Meats	0
Canned fish	0

Seafood	0
Poultry	0

Knowing about fructose and glycemic index will help you to remain constantly aware of any hidden sugars or any risks to your goals. A lot of people fail to cure their sugar addictions by turning unknowingly to substitutes such as dried fruits, fruit juices, and even starchy foods like rice cakes or crackers. This keeps their love of super sweet foods alive and nurtures the usual blood sugar patterns they have lived with for a long time.

When you understand that fructose appears in natural foods and that the glycemic index of foods will alter your blood sugar, you can really enjoy a lot more control over the outcome of your sugar detox program.

The final things to know about are the foods that you must not eat while trying to detox, and the "fake" sugars that are extremely harmful and problematic. Let's look at those forbidden foods first.

Forbidden Foods

You are probably well aware of the many things you need to cut from the diet, but let's just make a final, official, list to help you steer clear of all possible threats and risks. The foods that are forbidden to you during a sugar detox (and which you will want to avoid afterward) are:

- Anything that can possibly qualify as a sweetener - because these include a list of more than 250 modern additives we cannot provide them all here, but make a point of learning all of the names for sugar and checking any labels for them.

- Bread, crackers, cereal, tortillas, flour, baked goods, cake, cookies, etc.
- Most grains, including buckwheat, millet, etc.
- Alcohol of any kind
- Fruit juices - even when they are pure and fresh
- Simple carbs of any kind, including pasta, rice, etc.
- Bottled sauces and condiments that are often the worst forms of hidden sugar
- Most packaged, pre-made, processed foods. Above we told you to read labels, but also consider just eliminating all processed foods as a way to guarantee that you are not consuming hidden sugars of any kind.
- Foods you know to be high GI

It is not that complicated to skip hidden sugars once you understand how carbohydrates operate in the body. While you are going to easily know to skip the sugar in the morning coffee, you might not have previously realized that the box of "healthy" granola bars packed such a devastating punch to your health and your blood sugar.

Now that you understand that they are loaded with sugar in the form of added sugar, simple carbs, and even some dried fruit and chocolate, you will cut them from the diet. What about those sugar free cookies and candies? Are they allowed? This is the time to discuss the different fake sugars, and why these are "forbidden" too.

The Truth about Fake Sweeteners

So, if you cannot ingest the classic forms of sugar such as table sugar and all of the added sugars, can you swap them out for all of the fake sugars? The little pink packets, the boxes promising all natural sugar alternatives, and the blatantly chemical formulations? If they have no calories and no impact on blood sugar they should be good to use...right?

No. Let's first look at these fake sugars and then explain why they are also on the list of forbidden foods for those attempting to rid themselves of sugar.

It can be remarkably easy to get confused and overwhelmed by the sugar and sugar alternatives in the stores. The most common are:

- Stevia - this one is at the top of everyone's "healthy" sugar alternative due to the remarkable marketing that has gone on around it. However, it is not all that it is cracked up to be. When eaten in its natural form, it is an herb, and it is fairly safe. When used as a sugar substitute, it is a highly processed food that is stripped of any nutrient content. There are some studies suggesting that several of the "real sugar" substitutes can trigger insulin reactions, and you want to avoid this.

- Sucralose - known as Splenda among other brand names, this is not a sugar though its manufacturers patently indicate that it is made from it. Instead, it is one of the commonly chlorinated artificial sweeteners. Thus, it comes with the same long list of health risks as other common sugar fakers like aspartame and saccharin.

- Honey - this is another food we mentioned earlier but have to mention here as so many authors and experts suggest that honey makes a good sugar substitute. It doesn't. It is loaded with sugar and is an officially forbidden food.

- Sugar alcohols - the names that this one appears under are sorbitol, xylitol, glycerol, mannitol, and more. They are among the most popular of the fakes and are similar to sugar in a few ways. They are not actually completely absorbed by the body (though the majority is taken into the small intestine and is the reason that they can often lead to bloating, gas, and diarrhea in so many), and do have an impact on blood sugar. They also contain calories and have GI figures. For instance, sorbitol has a GI of 9 for every gram consumed. These are also much less sweet than sugar and require a great deal more to create a sweet flavor, so they must be avoided.

- Agave - we have touched on this one in earlier parts of the book but need to point out that agave syrup and other products are being touted as sugar substitutes. They pack a whopping 80% fructose and are just another form of sweetener. They are not sugar free and they are heavily processed, meaning that they are to be avoided at all costs.

The descriptions offer plenty of reasons to avoid these fakes, and then there are the following points to consider as well:

- Fake sugars are heavily processed. They are missing any sort of nutrient content and can have surprisingly high numbers of unpleasant side effects.

- They are chemicals, and that should be enough of a problem to steer people away from their use.

- They do not help you to curb your sugar craving. As an example, the popular powdered drinks that are sold in portable envelopes and which are sized for adding directly to a bottle of water are super sweet. The same can be said of the fake sugars used in sugar free candies. We've mentioned the problems with cutting sugar addiction and one of them is that you must stop eating foods that are your favorite sweets. How can you get past cravings when these super sweet alternatives exist? The truth is that most make it more difficult to bring sugar addiction to an end because they support rather than discourage your taste for sweets.

Thus, you must avoid the use of any and all varieties of fake sugar. They are all examples of chemically altered foods, which makes them harmful to health, but they are also reinforcing the taste or desire for hyper sweet foods. You cannot end the cycle of craving and of having a "commercially designed" palate if you use these substitutes.

The best choice is to leave them on the store shelves and slowly tune down the amped up taste for sugar that has been a lifetime in the making.

Interestingly enough, you will find that the fake sugars are something directly marketed to women more than men. Whether it is the pink packages of fake sugar, the little tubes of powdered drinks designed to fit into your purse, or the commercials showing smiling models gobbling down cupcakes made with artificial sugar it seems like there is a bit of a conspiracy at work.

The truth is that marketers know all about food preferences and understand that women actually crave sugar more than men. This can make it tough for the ladies of the world who are working to shake their sugar addictions, and this will allow us to now turn our attention to some of the sugary conspiracy theories (which are not so theoretical at all). This is the focus of the final chapter.

Chapter Four

Sweet Conspiracy Theories?

We may find in the long run that tinned food is a deadlier weapon than the machine-gun.
— George Orwell

Do women want more sugar than men? Is there really a government agenda where corn syrup is concerned? Why are experts steering us towards carbs even as an obesity epidemic occurs? What is with the USDA food pyramid anyway? And what on earth is the Coca Cola Conspiracy?
There are as many mysteries associated with the ways that sugar is pushed on the public as there are about aliens and JFK. So, is there any truth to them? Actually, the sad truth is that there is a lot of evidence that sugar is indeed something being pushed (just like a drug) on to the masses. Some of the pushing is just failed good intentions, but most if it has to do with one of the worst forces on the entire planet - greed. When partnered with scientific evidence, greed can become incredibly powerful, and where massive commercial food producers are concerned, sugar and greed add up to a lot of trouble.

Take as a prime example of the truth behind the many whispers of "conspiracy theory" in the food business, an article written for The New York Times in February of 2013. In "The Extraordinary Science of Addictive Junk Food" the author explains how global food giants (around eleven of them) work together to share their scientific discoveries about making snack foods more addictive.

While feeling pressure to conform to growing consumer and governmental demands to provide foods and meals that are more nutritious, the groups mentioned in the article also dedicated just as much (if not more) energy towards perfecting the addictive properties of their foods and learning how to best market them - and to whom.

For instance, consider the soft drink maker Coca Cola and their ongoing battle to remain available in public schools. They know their product is detrimental to health, that it can cause calcium depletion in kids, that it leads to tooth decay, and that it is a major contributor to obesity, and yet it markets to school age kids.

Conspiracy? Not a very well hidden one, but nonetheless a definite agenda that is against public welfare and all about the bottom line. We can see this repeatedly in the other food conspiracy theories, such as that marketing of sugar substitutes (as well as sugary foods) to women.

It's all in the Mind...

Food studies repeatedly demonstrate that men are fond of the salty and meaty snacks ranging from potato chips to beef jerky and it is women who head for cakes, cookies, candy and ice cream.

Why that is the case is an interesting issue. Several studies have revealed the following:

- Females tend to have a more pronounced desire for high calorie and high sugar foods.
- Females have a biological need to maintain their body fat at a specific percentage to ensure pregnancy (around 17 percent body fat is best) and a natural preference for high calorie and high sugar foods would encourage this to occur.
- Higher levels of estrogen trigger cravings for sweeter foods.
- Women have a lower level of serotonin in the brain, and in order to enjoy good sleep and a better mood they are going to experience cravings for the sugary and sweet foods that trigger this neurotransmitter to be manufactured.
- Women are more prone to anxiety and depression, and many experts believe that sugary and sweet food cravings are a form of self-medication.

Okay, you might say, women may be biologically programmed to savor the foods that are the sweetest and the most fattening. If that is the case, why not just eat them? In a nutshell, these foods are not going to promote good health. In fact, most are detrimental to good health. The fact that food makers create them by the score and that marketers identify and target the most likely audience does not negate the realities about these foods.

As an example, watch any commercial for fancy boxed chocolates. They rarely depict an overweight woman with an unhealthy complexion and health problems eating the chocolates. Instead, it is usually a gorgeous, slender woman who looks to be the picture of health - right down to her cavity free smile.

In the New York Times article mentioned above, one of the subjects admitted that "The selling of food matters as much as the food itself." That clearly indicates that any scientific evidence that any type of food will sell is going to encourage the manufacturers to abuse the information for their own profits.

You can see this in the ways that fast food chains market their meals for kids; the ways that one sandwich chain touts the health of its products even though most are heavily laden with carbs, sodium, and fat; and the way that alcoholic beverage companies show people consuming their products and really acting normal and staying healthy.

When you are seeking to bring your sugar addiction to an end, it is likely that you are going to become extremely aware of the many ways that sugar laden foods are pitched to the public. You might also begin to resent this sort of blatant marketing of addictive and unhealthy foods.

The one thing that you can do is to stop buying any of these products. Though your choice might seem like a veritable drop in the ocean, it is a sure way of protecting yourself and your good health from their destructive merchandise. Additionally, most people who eliminate sugar from their diet tend to see a huge drop in their monthly or weekly food expenses. This is because they will be making a lot of their own foods, avoiding fast foods and prepackaged meals, and generally eliminating a lot of waste in the budget.

There is also the savings that comes with improved health. Over the long term, a person who eliminates sugar from their diet is going to see radical improvements in their health. They cut risks of developing such issues as heart disease, diabetes, and obesity. This keeps a lot of money in their wallets and ensures that their healthcare costs are kept to a minimum too! Of course, you are more likely to find it easy to cut your consumption of sugary foods if you also understand that marketers are not the only "bad guys". We already mentioned that food companies work hard to create addictive foods, but there is even more to the story. They also work hard to create vicious cycles within addiction too.

Coca-Cola Conspiracy

If you browse around the Internet you will find that there are a lot of bloggers, food enthusiasts, and conspiracy theorists discussing the "Coke Conspiracy".

What is it? It is actually very annoying and is prone to make you want to walk around with a sandwich board encouraging everyone you know to cut their Coca Cola habit.

It begins in 1985…at that time Coca Cola ran a campaign for their newest product called "New Coke". While it actually flopped, there is something interesting about the experiment. The reason it was called "new" was because the recipe was altered quite substantially. If you read the label you would see that it contained much more sodium (salt) than Classic Coke, and it contained a lot more caffeine.

Now, you might reasonably wonder, why on earth would the makers of this world famous beverage decide to alter the recipe in this way? It is easy to explain if you look at the digestive science behind the beverage.

Coke, and other similar products, is made of carbonated water and a lot of sugar. There are some artificial colors and flavors, but for the most part it is all about the sweet and bubbly experience that occurs when you drink the stuff.

Now, that might be tolerable if all Coke contained was the fizzy water and sugar (and by tolerable we don't mean we agree with selling such a harmful beverage), but that is not the case.

The New Coke product revealed that the makers of the drink understood quite well that if you boost the amount of caffeine it increases the drinker's reaction to it. In other words, the more caffeine squeezed into that bottle of soda the more it acts as a stimulant and as a diuretic. This would make the person drinking the soda have to urinate a lot more. However, the new recipe also increased the amount of sodium.

Now, you might ask yourself why a sweet drink has a lot more salt. The answer is simple, salt makes you thirsty. If you consume a lot of sodium at the same time you guzzle down a diuretic, you are going to make yourself thirstier and thirstier. Additionally, all of that sugary sweetness is masking the horrible taste of the salt and triggering the many reactions we already know that sugar causes in the brain. It is like a liquid drug that creates ever greater intensities of thirst.

Let's consider this: When Coke was first created it came in a 6.5 ounce bottle. Today, it is easy to get your hands on a "big gulp", a 20 oz bottle and more. You drink this monster beverage and damage yourself with all of the corn syrup it uses as a sweetener (it used to use cane sugar, but that was not sweet enough for the evolving consumer demands for super sweetened foods nor cheap enough for the beverage maker). You spike your blood sugar by drinking a beverage with a GI of 100, by consuming far too much of it, and by enduring the many after effects.

It doesn't stop there because you are also consuming tremendous quantities of caffeine and sodium (there is 55 mg of sodium in a single can of Coke). These will force your body to give up a lot of fluid (taking a lot of nutrients along the way) and experience great thirst at the same time.

And by now you also know that sugar is triggering a lot of activity in your brain and that if you are already addicted to sugar you will have a higher tolerance for larger and sweeter servings of soda.

So, what it boils down to is that the Coca Cola Company's scientists and product designers understand the chemistry behind cravings and addiction. They use them to create products that consumers want, and continue to want even more after they use them. The soda industry is a billion dollar venture and makes vast fortunes every year.

However, since the 1970s, the soda industry has relied on another industry for its main ingredient - sugar. This is a very complex story, but one that is well worth knowing.

Corn Syrup Conspiracy

In 1966 a Japanese food scientist discovered HFCS or high fructose corn syrup. In the mid-1970s, this additive was introduced to the American food supply. It is much cheaper to grow (as it comes from corn) and it is 20% sweeter than other natural sweeteners like sugar cane and honey.

According to some studies, corn syrup in the SAD increased by more than ten thousand percent from the time it arrived in the markets in the 70s through the year 2006. In fact, it is estimated that most people consume around 65 pounds of it each year - even people who don't think they have a "sweet tooth".

This is because it appears everywhere. From hamburger buns and breakfast cereals to pickles and milk.

The reason for the explosive use for such a new ingredient is interesting and starts with American President Richard Nixon's war on poverty. In 1972 the president asked the USDA to help the country to find methods for lowering the cost of a healthy diet.

By the time that high fructose corn syrup became available, the USDA determined that most of the chronic diseases were the result of a high fat diet. By the early 1980s, both the USDA and the American Medical Association, the AMA, had advocated that diets be reduced from 40 to 30 percent fat and that the difference in calories and nutrients be made up of carbohydrates.

You are probably starting to understand where this is heading.

During this period of time it was also discovered that high fructose corn syrup was much better for companies looking to cut costs. This was good news to companies that made sugary foods such as candy and soda because the sugar market had been in a bit of a crisis since the early 1960s, when Castro assumed control of Cuba (and which meant that a huge chunk of the world's sugar supply was now gone).

This led to America's own sugar industry being developed in Florida, Hawaii, and Louisiana. However, within a decade, sugar cane was replaced by corn syrup. Not only was it cheaper, but it was sweeter and made from a crop in wild abundance - corn. It also "improved" the taste of the many "low fat" foods being promoted as healthier by the USDA and the AMA.

Note: At that time few people understood that fat stored in the liver would eventually make you get fatter. Instead, people blamed dietary fat as the leading cause of bodily fat too.

Then, a major hurricane in the 1980s destroyed what remained of the traditional Caribbean sugar crops and most American food makers were forced to turn to high fructose corn syrup supplies as a solution. This resulted in some enormous changes to both the corn and food industries. The result being that around 16% of all corn grown in the United States today is going to become high fructose corn syrup.

The abundance of this ingredient led many food makers to begin using it to enhance the palatability of their foods. Thus, it showed up for the first time in things like ketchup, salad dressing, traditionally unsweetened breads, and baby formulas.

Marketing and sales professionals also took note of the increase in sales as soon as the added sugars were used, and began to create more products to feed this growing addiction to sugar.

Today, we can see that a lot of agencies are seeking to reduce the power of the sugar and food industries. People like Mayor Bloomberg in New York City sought to make soft drinks an illegible item for purchase with food stamps. This is because his office recognized the direct connection between high sugar consumption and poor health.

Why would that ultimately matter? It is because diets high in sugar have been proven to be a leading cause of hypertension, obesity, diabetes, and other chronic diseases. Current estimates indicate that these issues cost roughly $147 billion (yes, that is billion) to treat, combat, and cure.

You and Sugar

So, if you take nothing else from reading the preceding pages, you should accept that it is up to you, and you alone, to protect your health. This is best done by eliminating all sources of harmful substances from your diet. Refined sugar is the primary cause of many enormous health concerns.

While your parents may have once warned you that too much sugar was going to rot your teeth, you have to also accept that it is a substance that is harmful to your body, your brain, and even your state of mind. It is not a natural material. You don't walk to a tree and pick sugar. It is a material made (mostly) from heavily processed corn. It takes nutrients from your body each time you eat it and it leaves behind a trail of destruction at the cellular level.

With all of this in mind, it is probably easier than ever to imagine giving up your sugar addiction. If you are still struggling with the idea, however, take some of these tips from health expert Robert Lustig who is currently writing a book about the dangers of sugar.

He says that the best things people can do for themselves is to:

- Cut sugar - in fact, he says "There is no reason for it...There is not one biochemical reaction in your body, not one, that requires dietary fructose, not one that requires sugar. Dietary sugar is completely irrelevant to life. People say oh, you need sugar to live. Garbage."
- Get exercise - you burn off the stored sugars when you challenge your body, and doing daily exercise is one way to help your body stabilize blood sugar and burn fat.
- Eat fiber - we already learned that it is not possible for your body to fully digest fiber, and it makes the body work to metabolize what it can. This gives you energy, nutrients, and keeps blood sugar stable.
- Use awareness with your diet - reading this book has already made you well aware of the need to cut out sugar and dramatically limit simple carbs. Keep up the awareness and keep learning about the best choices, such as removing all processed foods from your home and diet.
- Skip fructose if possible - this is not a safe food and should not appear in your diet except in the form of all natural fruits.
- Keep kids off this drug - if you have children or play a role in any child's life, try to keep them away from sugar in any form. The only sweetness that kids need (apart

from the love of their family and friends) is that found in natural, whole fruits.

In addition to these insightful suggestions, we also offer you some final tips for success with overcoming sugar addiction:

- Know the template - Always keep that food pyramid in mind. Start with healthy fats as your largest percentage of calories, then lean proteins, then the vegetables for fiber, and only then the tiniest amounts of simple carbs.
- Read labels but skip processed foods if you can - Unless it is entirely impossible to eat only whole foods just skip the canned and boxed foods. If you have to eat them - read the labels and skip everything with added sugar.
- Make a diet plan - Whether you begin with a journal and then draft formal plans, you need to make sure that you have at least one week of meals planned in advance of your transition to a sugarless lifestyle.
- Use exquisite timing - If you want that bit of fruit each day, try to consume it around 20 minutes after you have finished brisk exercise because your body is going to just gobble up the energy from the sugar at that point in time. There will be no chance that the sugar is going into storage. If you eat it with a bit of protein, you will optimize the muscle repair too.
- Modify as needed - If you are going to use a formal 21 day detox, don't force yourself down the path to failure

by refusing to modify the plan. For example, we mentioned that you can use fruit or even some starchy vegetables if you know it will get you past hurtles and temptations.

The key is moderation in modification. In other words, allow a bit of them if that is what will get you through a particularly difficult moment. Just consider doing something like partnering a cheat with a workout to consume the glucose and regulate the blood sugar as soon as possible.

- Create a list of reasons - Why did you choose to cut sugar? Is it because you don't want to be an addict? Is it because of the blatant wrongs being done by the food industry? Whatever your reasons, write them down, share them if you want, and keep them with you to remind you to persist in moments that might be trying.

- Focus on food - Becoming a no sugar person is a good time to also begin developing awareness of your palate. In other words, try to focus on your food. Don't watch TV as you eat. Don't distract yourself. Sit down, and be sure to really taste every bite. Over time, you will realize that your palate becomes more and more sensitive to flavors and only mildly sweet foods will satisfy your old sugar demons.

- If you cannot afford organic it is okay - Don't skip certain foods because you cannot afford or find organic. If there is no way of using grass fed and organic beef, as an example, just buy good quality cuts. It is more important to get that valuable protein than it is to skip it. Also, start exploring your town and region for farmer's markets as they are good resources for more affordable organics.

- Identify weakness - Do you eat for emotional reasons? Stress? Boredom? Because you are obsessed with a particular food? There are times when everyone eats too much of one thing. Know why you might binge on M&Ms or potato chips, and create a plan of action to overcome it.

- Go slow if it helps - Can't commit to a fully sugarless lifestyle? That's okay; you can just try to take it in stages. For instance, for one week just eat sugarless breakfasts. Then a week later add a sugarless snack. It may take more than a month to get there, but you might be able to more easily transition this way than to do the 21 day challenge.

- Weigh yourself - Even if weight loss is not a goal of cutting sugar, you are going to be astonished at how fast you drop the pounds when you do follow a 21 day detox. You are eating hundreds (and perhaps thousands) of calories each week in the form of sugar and simple carbs. Cutting them is going to allow you to shed weight in many ways - fat stored in the organs, water weight from the toxicity of sugar, and weight loss from daily exercise.

- Fall down and get back up - You may not make it the first time you try to cut the sugar. It is okay. Just keep trying. You will get there.

That last one is the most important. This chapter has shown you that the cards are stacked against those who want to permanently eliminate sugar from their diets. It is everywhere and it is offered up on TV, on the radio, and in every type of advertisement.
It is a drug used by modern society and it is incredibly hard to get rid of, but you can do it if you use the tips in this book.

In Conclusion...

Addiction to sugar is real. Whether you use a formal sugar detox as described in this book, or you just gradually eliminate all sources of refined sugar and simple carbs from your diet, you will benefit greatly from the choice and the effort.

Sugar is a drug that acts just like all of the world's other drugs. It creates a rush of pleasure chemicals in the brain and it allows us to become tolerant to it. This creates the need for ever more of the drug to get the same response. When you cut this drug from your diet, you experience classic signs of withdrawal that range from emotional outbursts and depression to physical symptoms like headache and digestive upset.

Be prepared for this, and be ready to combat the worst of the challenges because you are only doing yourself a lot of good by cutting out sugar from your life. You will want to find others who are experiencing the same issues that you are, and who have decided to stand against the pervasive poisoning of the general public through the "pushing" of sugar.

Fortunately, this is something that is becoming more and more common. For the first time in decades, the public is paying attention to the sugar issue. People are talking about controversies associated with sugar and the marketing of sugary foods. They are aware that sugar is being added to everything, and entirely for the profit of the corn and food suppliers.

People are not meant to be trained pets who eat only what is supplied to them, and your decision to cut your sugar addiction proves that you understand the importance of making good choices. Your health is in your hands, and just removing sugar is going to improve it dramatically.

We wish you the best of luck in your journey to freedom from sugar addiction. You will have many interesting experiences along the way, but the one you will enjoy the most is waking for the first time knowing that your body is free of something that may have been clouding your mind, altering your perception, and impacting the quality of your life.

Once you are free of sugar and simple carbs, you won't want to go back to eating them. Instead, you will taste flavors as you never have before and discover what it means to be truly healthy.

"Each patient carries his own doctor inside him."
— Norman Cousins, Anatomy Of An Illness

Works Cited

Baldwin, A. (2012). *Transcript: Here's the Thing: Robert Lustig.* Retrieved 2013, from WNYC: http://www.wnyc.org/shows/heresthething/2012/jul/02/transcript/

Cole, R. (2008). *21 Day Sugar Detox.* Retrieved 2013, from Rosecole.com: http://www.rosecole.com/handouts/21DaySugarDetox.pdf

Dolson, L. (2008). *Fructose - Sweet But Dangerous.* Retrieved 2013, from About: http://lowcarbdiets.about.com/od/nutrition/a/fructosedangers.htm

Ford, A. (2013). *Why Do Women Love Sugar?* Retrieved 2013, from Divine Caroline: http://www.divinecaroline.com/self/wellness/why-do-women-love-sugar-truth-about-your-sweet-tooth

Gebel, E. (2011). *How the Body Uses Carbohydrates, Proteins, and Fats.* Retrieved 2013, from Diabetes Forecast: http://forecast.diabetes.org/magazine/features/how-body-uses-carbohydrates-proteins-and-fats

Healthy Living. (n.d.). *Glycemic Index.* Retrieved 2013, from Healthy Living 2008: http://www.healthy-living.org/html/glycemic_index_table.html

Jegtvig, S. (2013). *How Much Added Sugar Can I Eat a Day?* Retrieved 2013, from About: http://nutrition.about.com/od/askyournutritionist/f/howmuchsugar.htm

Kovaks, J. (2013). *How to Increase Your Metabolism and Start Losing Fat.* Retrieved 2013, from WebMD: http://www.webmd.com/diet/features/increase-your-metabolism-start-losing-fat

Mercola, J. (2010). *76 Dangers of Sugar to Your Health.* Retrieved 2013, from Dr. Mercola: http://articles.mercola.com/sites/articles/archive/2010/04/20/sugar-dangers.aspx

Moss, M. (2013). *The Extraordinary Science of Addictive Junk Food.* Retrieved 2013, from NYT: http://www.nytimes.com/2013/02/24/magazine/the-extraordinary-science-of-junk-food.html?pagewanted=all&_r=0

Repinski, K. (2011). *How Sugar Ages Your Skin.* Retrieved 2013, from Prevention: http://www.prevention.com/beauty/beauty/how-sugar-ages-your-skin

Rosedale, R. (2008). *Be a Fat Burner.* Retrieved 2013, from Healthy Living: http://www.healthy-living.org/html/be_a_fat_burner.html

SELF Nutrition Data. (2013). *Glycemic Index.* Retrieved 2013, from Self Nutrition Data: http://nutritiondata.self.com/topics/glycemic-index#glycemic

Toad. (2012). *How to Complete the 21 Day Sugar Detox with Ease.* Retrieved 2013, from Primal Toad: http://primaltoad.com/sugar-detox-tips/

Van Allen, J. (2013). *Kick Your Sugar Addiction .* Retrieved 2013, from Shine: http://shine.yahoo.com/healthy-living/kick-sugar-addiction-9-simple-steps-152600441.html

Natural Healing College Authors (2013) Alternative Medicine Treatments: The Holistic Health Practitioner seeks to take care of the root causes of disease, rather than merely eliminating or suppressing the symptoms

Voiland, A. (2012). *10 Things the Food Industry Doesn't Want You to Know.* Retrieved 2013, from US News and World Report - Health: http://health.usnews.com/health-news/articles/2012/03/30/things-the-food-industry-doesnt-want-you-to-know

Is sugar toxic? by: CBSNEWSONLINE Dr. Sanjay Gupta reports on new research showing that beyond weight gain, sugar can take a serious toll on your health, worsening conditions ranging from heart disease to cancer.

WebMD. (2012). *Sugar Addiction: Symptoms, Cravings, Detox, and Diet Tips.* Retrieved 2013, from WebMD: http://www.webmd.com/diet/ss/slideshow-sugar-addiction

wiseGeek. (2013). *What is Metabolism?* Retrieved 2013, from wisegeek: http://www.wisegeek.com/what-is-metabolism.htm

Reference Books:
Alternative-Medicine -The-Definitive-Guide
-by-Larry-Trivieri-Jr-9781587611414
Anatomy-and-Physiology-for-Dummies
-by-Maggie-Norris-9780470923269
Ayurvedic-Cooking-for-Westerners-by
-Amadea-Morningstar-9780914955146
Ayurvedic-Yoga-Therapy-by
-Mukunda-Stiles-9780940985971
Becoming-Raw
-by-Brenda-Davis-9781570672385
Complete-Food-and-Nutrition
-Guide-by-Roberta-Duyff-9780470041154
Encyclopedia-of-Herbal-Medicine
-by-Andrew-Chevallier-9780789467836
Essentials-of-Anatomy
-by-Valerie-C-Scanlon-9780803622562
Fitness-and-Health
-by-Brian-Sharkey-9780736056144
Food-Cures
-by-Joy-Bauer-9781609613129
Foods-to-Fight-Cancer
-by-Richard-Beliveau-9780756628673
Healing-with-Vitamins
-by-Editors-of-Rodale-Health-Books-9781594868061
Internal-Cleansing
-by-Linda-Berry-9780761529323

Nutrition-for-Life
-by-Lisa-Hark-9780756626235
Prescription-for-Dietary-Wellness
-by-Phyllis-Balch-9781583331477
Prescription-for-Herbal-Healing
-by-Phyllis-Balch-9780895298690
Prescription-for-Nutritional-Healing
-by-Phyllis-Balch-9781583334003
Secrets-of-the-Pulse
-by-Vasant-Lad-9781883725136
Textbook-of-Ayurveda-Vol-1
-by-Vasant-Lad-9781883725075
Textbook-of-Ayurveda-Vol-2
-by-Vasant-Lad-9781883725112
The-Complete-Book-of-Chinese-Health-and-Healing
-by-Daniel-Reid-9781570620713
The-Herbal-Drugstore
-by-Linda-White-9781579547059
The-Herbal-Medicine-Makers-Handbook
-by-James-Green-9780895949905
The-Human-Body-Book
-by-Steve-Parker-9780756628659
The-New-Detox-Diet
-by-Elson-Haas-9781587611841
the-worlds-healthiest-foods
-by-George-Mateljan-9780976918547
The-Yoga-of-Herbs
-by-David-Frawley-9780941524247
Vitamins-Herbs-Minerals
-by-H-Winter-Griffith-9781555612634

Weight Loss by Quitting Sugar and Carb

Learn How to Overcome Sugar Addiction - A Sugar Buster Super Detox Diet

ISBN-13:978-1494449285

ISBN-10:1494449285

FREE Bonus Offer: free recipes and other health and wellness related books

Please Click Here for Instant Access to Free Recipe Book
http://www.healthylifenaturally.com/quitsugar/

Other Recommended Reads:

I Quit Sugar Cookbook

Your Complete 8-Week Detox Program

Is Sugar Toxic?

You've been provided with a perfect body to house your soul for a few brief moments in eternity. So regardless of its size, shape, color, or any imagined infirmities, you can honor the temple that houses you by eating healthfully, exercising, listening to your body's needs, and treating it with dignity and love.- Dr. Wayne Dyer

Made in the USA
Middletown, DE
07 November 2014